LAND OF OPHIR

DELUKE MUWANIGWA

ISBN:
Hardbound-978-621-470-661-7
MOBI/KINDLE-978-621-470-662-4
Softbound/Paperback-978-621-470-663-1

Published by:
Poetry Planet Book Publishing House
Rosario, Pozorrubio, Pangasinan, Philippines
Contact Number: 09554960094
Email: maritesritumalta@gmail.com

ACKNOWLEDGMENTS

I would like to dedicate this collection of poetry to Barbara, my wife, and my two grown up kids, Dananayi and Mudiwa Nathasia.

To my Philippines publisher, particularly Madam Dr. Marites (Tess) Ritumalta and her team. I want to thank her for hosting and managing the Ophir Awards of 2022 at which I was conferred with an honorary DLitt and FOWr awards. Also, a big thank to my fellow poets on Poetry Planet Book Publishing House.

Kevin of Allpoetry.Com for encouraging me to keep writing by posting some of my poems as "Front page picks". This had the tremendously powerful effect of encouraging me to write some more.

And, of course, to my Publishers and Printers, a big thanks to you all.

Definition of Ophir: a biblical land of uncertain location but reputedly rich in gold.

The Philippines is the Ancient and Biblical Land of Gold, Ophir.

Ophir is a port or a region mentioned in the Bible, famous for its wealth. King Solomon is supposed to have received shipments of gold, silver, sandalwood, precious stones, ivory, apes and peacocks, every three years. The location of Ophir is a mystery even today. There is much speculation as to where this place is.

Zimbabwe is the legendary land of Ophir, the ancient country that enriched the kingdoms of Hiram, Solomon, and Sheba with gold and ivory thousands of years ago. It is also home to the magnificent Victoria Falls, the mighty Zambezi River and Hwange National Park, one of Africa's best safari destinations"

In August,2022, we met in the Philippines for a literature symposium, at which literati from all over the world showcased their literary works. Covid 19 restrictions caused some to participate virtually by doing a ten-minute video showcasing published works.

I did my video by presenting my six published books, dressed in my national colours and recited my poem "Hwange National Park" and lastly, I wrote the poem "We Met in The Land of Ophir"'

I was awarded an Honorary DLitt and an FOWr at the end of the symposium.

I hope readers of this poetry book will enjoy it and hopefully be inspired to become poets.

TABLE OF CONTENTS

WE MET IN THE LAND OF *OPHIR*

We met in the Land of Ophir
from all over the world we converged
shared awards and poems without fear
and hope those who are not poets and writers
are converted

When a poet laments the world cries
when a poet laughs the world smiles
when a poet recites a poem time flies
when a poet reads a poem it is heard for miles

Poetry brings the world together
poetry in any language speaks the same tongue
poetry resonates to one and all forever
the four corners of the earth it will touch

It preaches peace in times of war
reminds us "We are the world"
encouraging all races, all faces, to meet some
more
sharing our experiences with peaceful words

My heart is teapot shaped
like my country
by dint of my progenitors
My head like Africa
by dint of King Nyatsimba Mutota
My pith is melanin
not quite pitch black.

In my veins and arteries runs blood in all direc-
tions
Eastwards like the Zambezi River
Southwards like the Save
Westwards like the Limpopo
and Northwards like the Gwayi
carrying life sustaining fish
whose totem is my identity.

The food I eat is so good
The Mopane tree concocting delicacies of tasty
creepy crawlies
The Baobab such dry fruity nuggets I shall not
want
My home is built upon a rock
it's construction timeless
The house of stone.
I am Zimbabwe

A Malawian genius died in Coventry, the
UK, in twenty eleven
I am sure there was work for him in heaven
I am sure such African brain is needed
even in the firmament
It's a pity his illustrious life here on earth
could not be permanent.
It's a pity here on earth
We were hardly told of his death

Had he been of the Aryan race
We would, ad nauseum, have seen his face
In newspapers
In bold letters
On the internet
On billboards on the interstate

Racism aside, this man was a genius
His contribution to science serious
He designed nuclear reactors in Britain, Ja-
pan and South Africa
A man bred, raised, educated and
groomed in Malawi, in Africa
Was Director of Engineering at British Aer-
ospace
His patents even flying on jet aircraft and
the shuttle to space.

He designed a gadget for detecting tu-
mours
And these are not rumours
He designed the Harrier Jump jet.
But, mention he doesn't get
Fixed design flaw which caused Chernobyl
disaster
Was awarded Galileo Award in Ninety
Eighty as a master.

His name is Professor Landson Mhango
A native of Malawi there in the jungle
Let's celebrate his astonishing accom-
plishments
His world changing achievements
And posthumously acknowledge
The power of knowledge
And commit ourselves as poets to embrace
the good in all humans
And not be blinkered by politicians and
stereotyping arguments.

YOU

You have been long gone from me
you decided to go your way
and I,
left on my own without you

You said I look elsewhere
in this fertile forest
you were now with cancer
not even death could separate you

I am lost without you in this forest called life
having tried to wander in it
alone
to the extent it has become my only home

There is a mist hanging over the limits of my
mind
preventing me seeing the wood from the trees
and clearly distinguishing my path to happiness
all pathways leading nowhere without you

You went somewhere
there,
decided to die and leave without me
leaving me to cry and live without you.

Even when you lay there

wasted
bald headed
unable to keep food down
I loved you to the end of the world
the end coming too soon
you succumbed
and I am numbed
missing you missing me
you,
missing me missing you

I needed to be someplace else really fast
the quickest way being to ensconce myself
in a metal cage
whose Gaussian surface is supported on
four rubber circular pivots and whose inte-
rior is padded with such comforts as to
cause me to want to sleep therein.

Once positioned in a bucket like seat feel-
ing smooth to my backside and bracing my
back and shoulders comfortably, I set
about inserting a miniature saw-toothed
dagger in a mysterious cave with bronze
stalagmites and stalactites which flexibly
made way for the blade
and on turning the small dagger clockwise,
my metal contraption came alive, various
lights coming on before it roared to life.

First, I placed my hands on a circular metal
bar padded with black felting, then moved
a guided lever on the floor of my vessel
from position P, through position N to D
and felt a primal urge to want to move, re-
straining my craft by stepping on a flat
pedestal, which, when I removed my foot
to place on another adjacent pedestal

caused my steel beast to rave and rant.

The only lever restraining it was one jutting opportunely out of the floor near my arm. I used my thump to press a knob on the centre of the stick out of the floor and pushed it down and the trees outside my steel cage starting moving backwards, first, slowly, then, gradually moving so fast that I busied myself working the padded wheel in order to avoid trees jumping in front of my contraption.

In no time I ended up some place else really fast.

GOOD OLD DAYS

The youth of today
would rather play
be gay
and we the parents should have nothing to say.

These are the leaders of tomorrow
who will bring the world so much sorrow
shirking responsibility
at every possibility.

The youth of today have so many rights
taking flight
whenever things are difficult
they are like a different cult
a different culture
causing societal rupture

In our good old days
I am not embarrassed to say
our old fashioned parents
made it apparent
their wish was our command
we had to do their demand
no questions asked
otherwise we were taken to task
the rod was our friend
beatings a normal trend.
the long can was never spared
and we, never scared

we got beat
for any of these

"Crying too long after being beaten
Not crying after being beaten
Crying without being beaten

Standing where elders are sitting
Sitting while elders are standing
Walking around aimlessly where elders are seated

Eating food prepared for visitors
Refusing to eat
Coming back home after sunset

Eating at the neighbour's home
Generally being too moody
Generally being too excited

Fighting even if you had no choice
Losing a fight with older age mate
Winning a fight with your age mate

Eating too slowly
Eating too quickly
Eating too much

Not finishing your food
Finishing your food and scraping your plate
Eating and talking

Sleeping while elders in the house have already wok-
en up
Looking at the visitors while they are eating
Looking at an elder eye ball to eye ball

When an elder is talking to you and you blink
When an elder is talking to you and you stare and
not blink
When you look at an elder through the corner of
your eye

When your mates are playing street football and you
join them
When your mates are playing and you don't join
them
Stumbling and falling when walking

When you don't wash your dish after eating
When you wash your dish improperly
When you almost break your dish

When you break your dish
When you bite your nails.
When you don't bath.

When you bath too quickly
When you take too long to bath.
When you're beaten in school for misbehaving
When a car almost knocks you down
When a car knocks you down and you don't die.
For not answering when spoken to

For answering back when spoken to.
For going to Church or Mosque late.
For borrowing shoe/wears from friends.

And giving salt or a needle to neighbors without
permission."

These were the good old days
full of discipline all the way.

INTIMATE BLISS

You are the Bermuda Triangle I miss
the forbidden bliss
only for me
immersive
mysteriously deep
a place I lose myself
forever lost
without trace
coming face to face
with the vortex of your affinity
your feminity
taking me to infinity
lost
to be found only by you
where mountains spew milk
fountains ooze honey
kissing an elixir
I am lost in you
It's nothing new
my love living in you
the Bermuda Triangle I miss
My intimate bliss

JUST INTENSE

I am a bit of a scatter brain,
my thoughts wandering all over the place,
unrestrained
unconstrained,
so much so that sometimes I see connections;
unrelated things becoming intertwined,
related stuff unbundled,
at the end of the day,
leaving my interlocutors in dismay.

I am misunderstood,
labelled rude,
but I wish people would appreciate
what they hear
feel
and see
is an iota of what really goes on in my mind.

If you could take a stroll in the avenues of my brain
you would never find your way out,
the name of every pathway labelled "No through
road"
and at every cul de sac,
bits of thoughts which really suck.

If you could swim in my mind,
it would not matter whether you crawled,
breast stroked
or simply trod water,

the end result would be the same,
sinking in a quagmire of thoughts far removed from
reality.

It is only when the bits and bytes
in my mind coalesce into words,
words flow to my index finger
and find life in a poem,
that's the time I make sense
showing I am not really dense.
I am just intense.

FUN IN THE SUN WITH THE SUN IS NO PUN

All energy is from the sun
Fossil fuels are due to the distance of the earth
from the sun
Hydropower from climate patterns due to the
sun
When there is need for power let's face the sun

How good it is now we can get power direct
from the sun
Power stations being wasteful and polluting
put a panel on the roof for power direct from
the sun
Global warming is stalling hydropower
put a panel get direct power from the sun
Reliability is excellent each installation talk-
ing direct to the sun.

What will it take to make people go to the
sun?
Power utilities give notice high tariffs
in five years to send customers to the sun
Government, local and rural authorities
force people to look to the sun
Quality solar accessories made in bulk
making it cheaper to talk to the sun.

All homes, small offices, churches, small
businesses getting power direct from the

sun
All small scales farms, gardens, horticulture
getting power direct from the sun
Power grids making money from higher
non socialist tariffs direct from the sun
Heavy industry with enough power for
growth from reliable grids all thanks to the
sun

There is nothing more guaranteed than the
sun
Life guaranteed by the sun
Profit guaranteed by the sun
Fun in the sun with the sun is no pun.

A BLESSING TO BE ALIVE

I been too busy playing God of late
worrying about why humans are the way
they are
worrying that the rains are late
that the war in Asia is still raging threaten-
ing the whole world
I failed to see the mango trees flowering
the weather changing in subtle barely per-
ceptible ways
only today
looking outside my front door
there was rain water all over the external
floor
I saw green mangoes almost ripening
felt the hope brought in by flashes of
lightning
shrouds of continuous gray clouds
and the guttural conversations of the
heavens
and with these observations
I realised the futility of playing God.
This world is bright even in the darkest
moments
beautiful in spite of the hatred of one for
another
This world is most hopeful when all seems
lost

at all cost
strive to stay alive
It is a blessing to be alive.

A RACK AND PINION

Of course, like a rack and pinion
I do have a definite opinion
My final position
not necessarily with the opposition.
There are days my point is to the left
when empathy is felt
days it's to the right
ready for a fight
Sometimes center
I am a dissenter
Sometimes I am in limbo
like a gringo
waiting for events
to prevent
finding myself stuck in a rut.
patience is a must.
For I must always be aware of the helix turning
the pain could be burning
your finger in the wrong place
and you, screwing your face
or going the opposite way
that day
the heavy job in the jaw
could drop, crush your toe
when you alter your position
by imposition.
It's a wonder how many have been killed

fatally squeezed
careless statements
by careless statesmen
dropping jaws
causing wars
and yet if you go deep
and balance you keep
we all want the same product
we are all pro life
but out of careless workmanship
the vice becomes a device for brinkmanship
whose calibrations
affect civilisations
causing unrest
beyond the bench
Notwithstanding all this
I try to do my bit
try to keep an open mind
you will find
I do have a definite opinion
like a rack and pinion

NO MORE!

This morning the train took off without me
again
toot tooting away leaving me on the
wrong footing
again
overhauling my plans for the day in spite
of how I feel
again
the smoke from the coal train clouding my
eyes with soothing.
again

At the point I go to sleep I remind myself
to keep an open mind and pray
Praying that the events of today see an in-
cremental improvement the next day I pray
Even set my clock to wake me up on time
for my morning prayer
but it seems the day itself conspires
against me for my prayer fails to stop the
train
the smoke from the coal train clouding my
eyes with soothing.
again

The train is not the issue though
No
I have two cars parked at home
so, the train is never the issue
No
The issue is that whenever I plan, whatever
I plan seems my answer ends up the same
A big No!
I am getting to a point where I should also
answer the same
and organise my life independent of the
time imposed by others
and say No!
No more!

NOT A DULL MOMENT

There's not a dull moment in my life
whenever I am at a loose end
when I am alone without a friend
I look around for things I like
even things I dislike are fair game
then, I try to describe the emotions evoked in
me
by the real life things I see
and in no time I write a poem
string some words for them,
those of a similar ilk whose emotional hunger for
imagery
is not imaginary
or immune to the life we live.
There's not a dull moment in my life
inspiration for me derives from sitting still
looking around me
typing a word on my phone without worrying
about where it will lead me
and that singular word seems to bring more
words
words opening more worlds
eventually my mind spontaneously combusting
an image
spawning ideas
ideas begetting ideas
and living with the satisfaction of creating some-

thing from nothing.
So, I am never lonely
I can't be lonely
some of the busiest and noisiest times of my life
are immersed in silence
those times I go places without moving an inch
times I relish building illusions into allusions
delusions into reality
for, for my sanity
I need the vanity
There's not a dull moment in my life.

Where I came from is farther than where I
go
It makes sense suffering the last ten miles
the burden, though, has become unbeara-
ble
Sometimes I feel like turning back sixty
miles
thinking it would be better
because things are now truly helter skelter.

Those who swore to be by my side all the
way
they seem to have developed self-inflicted
swollen feet
swollen due to hours hobnobbing with un-
known individuals
lending ears to everyone they meet
Now they say they want to disembark
"You can go alone!" they remark

I am not sure I can brave the steep hills
and lakes with snakes of the last ten miles
nor am I sure it's even ten miles to go,
it could be fifteen
I am not sure I am welcome where I go
or that there won't be so much silence and
desolation I shall wish I had chosen anoth-

er route.
I am now full of doubt.

I am now wise in hindsight too late to
know
a man is born alone no matter the sweet
words of those you meet
that, there are journeys of no return in
which in turn every milestone is your first
and last
that, there is no point in explaining yourself
as no one really pays attention
the best is to drop a poem a mile
hoping someone will read your story,
understand and smile long after you are
gone.

Today is one of those days
I have nothing to say
Nothing new
like I have no point of view
This is quite unusual
because it is a ritual
to always have a mind
you find
even about a non-event
I have to vent
a silly story
turning gory
metaphors
cater for
the lack of content
to the extent
something
comes out of nothing.
Today I am a failure
in my area
of expertise
I am not at ease
words fail me
I fail to be
the scribe
who would describe
a vacuum as an event

or at least attempt
to turn silence to noise
being prostate into a poise
draw tears
from ears
and for years
hears
what others don't
or won't
I hear rhymes
all the time
categories of allegory
prosody in glory
in clear notes
by rote
from memory
through perjury
or anyhow
doesn't matter how
but not today
I have nothing to say.
Nothing at all
although
last night I hit a pedestrian
standing off centreline dressed in black like an
alien
a glancing blow
I know
just my rear view mirror

I stopped to see if he was injured
a bit of pain on backside
refused a ride
to get painkillers
gave him cash to find other healers
I suspected
I expected
a bottle of beer
it was clear
he had been drinking
and I was thinking
it was my lucky day
he was just grazed
it could have been worse
finding the words
to explain the incident
the accident
I should have so much to say
today
but, today is one of those days
I have nothing to say.

I am coming to the end of my poems
prematurely
before the plot reaches a climax
before the mass of disjointed ideas is con-
joined into one organic entity.
I am not sure what the therapy to this most
debilitating condition is.
Some say I should take it slow but I don't
know.
that, I should read more than I write
but, doing a line or two a day may make
me lose interest in the theme.
Some say, whenever the ideas are not
coming fast and furious I should retire to
bed, but I am curious as to whether the
same feeling will still be with me the next
day. I am assured the contraption which
assumes the shape of my body
promising me respite from the rigours of
carrying myself and my ideas will rejuve-
nate me no end,
the one which aligns my feet and head
horizontally in the hope my inspiration on
the morrow will come to reality as profuse-
ly promised by the makers of these plat-
forms, but try as much as I can there is no
improvement in the flow even after resting

my head.
I am still coming to the end of my poems
prematurely. Sadly, it may be time to admit
the lack of resonance in my craft. To finally
admit the paucity of ideas. The impotence
of the messages and simply that I am po-
etically daft.

DEATH BE DEAD

Death become silent in the middle of the living
for your hand is not fashioned for giving
Your temper not for sympathy
demeanour not for empathy
You steal at unexpected moments
without a word or comment
without shame
your aim
To dominate living loving mortals
with thick walls of your silent portal
Death be dead
you fill me with dread.
Death be dead
get out of my head
Let me move on ahead
Death be dead.

Pity is, if you go round the city
you will not find anybody lonelier than a
poet.
someone so maladjusted to fitting in
the only companions are the poems he
writes.
It's not right.
there are brothers and sisters
so called friends
even a wife
but his marriage of convenience to his po-
ems seems to fill in the void,
the void devoid of human companionship,
where at night heavens are littered with
sta-nzas,
and to get some peace in the cosmos the
last ship to the launch pad is the SS Verses
where a balanced diet is a recital of bal-
lads.
There are other lonely beings
the madman going from bin to bin
the soldier in battle cut off from his com-
rades
left with one grenade
many lonely souls
but if you go round the city
you will not find anybody lonelier than a

poet. Hail I him.
Thank God, poetry does exist,
otherwise rulers of man would be forced to
chant "Death to the infidel", thinking there
is a rebellious treason,
not knowing the reason is there is a lonely
space where conversations with the soul
can only be done through poetry.

FACELESS SOULS

They give me hope
like Joanna
these faceless souls I meet
never on the street
hidden behind the luminous screen of my phone
They come to my home
dismembered into ones and zeros
my heroes
coming straight to my room
on digital brooms
I love them so
and like Nigerians
they keep saying they love me more
every poem I send
getting me a new friend
another faceless soul
that's not all
I am elated to teleport my thoughts
though fraught
with so many Bantu assumptions
I am not put under sanctions
the faceless souls
becoming trolls
Seems they are not rigid
kindness runs in their digits
in their blood
I am so so glad

Went round to collect my first self-
published poetry book at the printers,
"Mbiresaurus",
and as expected,
I was asked to sit in reception while they
tied up loose ends
and I did what I do when at a loose end
looked around the reception for inspira-
tion.

It was pretty much a run of the mill recep-
tion without much artistic conception, lack-
ing thrills, but for me, looking through the
doorway at the greenery outside was more
awe inspiring, seeing the conversations of
green from dark to light
and every hue in-between,
the beauty being each hue knew exactly its
place in the green scheme of things for
perfect self-expression
so much so that their impression to me
brought calmness
a feeling which not long after made me
feel I belonged,
this was my life publishing poetry books,
this is what I liked,
not minding the awkward looks I got from

the receptionist and staff at the printers of-
fice.

I could tell the lady's curiosity was peaking
and anytime she would be speaking
and soon she cracked
"How long have you been writing poetry?"
"How do you think of these poems?"
"What drives you to write poetry?"

I don't remember answering any of these
questions and I doubt she really wanted
me to answer seeing how rapidly the que-
ries came flying and me, busy trying not to
be intimidated by the picture of our Presi-
dent on the reception wall,
tall,
imposing,
ever so present,
as if he will ask what you have done as a
patriot
where your vote was and where it will be
the national elections coming fast.

Reflections may be mixed
due to some deflection missed
so that what you see is not what you get
and you may be forced to change your mind set
I wish I had control of my own reflection
so that what I see is a spitting image of my res-
urrection
unfortunately what people think they see
and what I think I see is not me
I keep telling them to see me in my writings
not rely on the ambience of lighting
for, in my poetry is where I am found
where an understanding of me is profound
they prefer the persona in their minds
leaving hidden mannerisms behind
much like looking in a shattered mirror
whose mixed images are of different eras
believing the many images are me
when what they see
are mixed reflections
distorted by mixed deflections.
and yet, the best reflections of me are free
hidden in plain sight for all to read
formed
in my poems

My eyes are on their knees
begging to see you
hands quivering
ready to hold you
arms already curved
ready to wrap around you.
legs swollen stiff
standing for hours
trying to find a way to you
lips developing a lisp
calling your name
My nose thinks of roses
ears drop tears
I long to hear you
teeth cutting my tongue
calling your name
it's not a game
these things I do
cause of you.
because I love you
I want you to know
I love you so.

FEAST YOUR EYES

Today my poem falls where it lies
a product of a lazy Saturday
this 19th day of November, 2022
the year is creeping towards the finale
looking back at the last year
poetry has stood by me
as I have it
never letting me down a bit.
I had sworn to write one a day
egged on by the encouraging comments on All-
Poetry
but just as I had sworn to eat only poultry
there are days I failed to write a poem
and days I wrote several.
I have written so many poems I have lost count
but it's not the amount
but the quality of these
which will please
but I am so far gone in this pursuit
I have to find time to suit
the demands of writing
and rightly,
today my poem falls where it lies
Poets on AllPoetry, please, feast your eyes.

Granted
Life goes on
for the life of me
it would be way more efficient
I would be way more proficient
with better coordination
and less subordination
The right hand knows not what does the left
having failed the ambidexterity test
the left only good for grabbing air
while the right takes its fair share.
and yet it is intuitive
if only the left and right worked hand in glove
showing love
hand in hand
I understand
I could achieve much more
what's more
it is not only the fault of my hands
even dastardly brigands
my feet are found one in retreat
the other intrepid
I find myself nowhere somewhere
somehow always failing somewhat
blaming someone else
instead of the incontinence of my limps
their insistence to be on a limp when I need

them most
Then I remember those who lost limps
those born without
amputees
Life goes on
Granted.

POEMS STOP

At some point they are there
like something to pluck in the air
then they stop
just like that
like there is a traffic light
only showing red
poems stop without being read.

Poetry is still there
though the poems stop
because poetry is life
as long as there is life
poetry will exist
even without the poems

For,
no one knows what a poem really is
not until it is read
even then
different readers will have different interpreta-
tions
some will laud
some won't
and although it will be part of poetry
it may not be a poem

For,

what really is a poem?
Just because it is said to be,
is it?

A poem is when a few words give
an emotion
a feeling
then understanding

words make one turn away
in wonder
look away
and acknowledge without a word
the simplicity.

A poem is the truth you cannot dodge
simply put
it means you dodge the truth
doing poetry
without poems
when poems stop.

Sometimes the day gets moody
brooding about the night being longer
when light is supposed to be stronger
than darkness
In the harshness
forgetting what goes around
will turn about
that the amount
of bounty
is related to the season
is the reason
But for me
I am free
whatever is the weather
whether
dark or light
dusk or twilight
I am too blessed
to be stressed
I like my sustenance
sizzling
with seasoning
whenever
and whatever's
the metaphysical misunderstanding.

I CAN'T SAY I WASN'T AFRAID

I can't say I wasn't afraid
standing before the Chief
speaking truth to power
an unfriendly audience
He brought strangers to shame me
to harass
embarrass me
I can't say I wasn't afraid
I kept my cool
even as they treated me like a fool
making me state the same fact
over and over
it became obvious
I was being unjustly persecuted
like a martyr prosecuted
to be executed
I can't say I wasn't afraid.
They tried reverse psychology
bad cop good cop
reminded me I was before decorated people
chairpersons of provincial assemblies
people in the national assembly
the senate
influential with money
I can't say I wasn't afraid.
They gave dire scenarios
exaggerated to dramatic effect

in my mind
unopened wounds already bled
someone already dead
but my statement remained the same
though I stammered
"I can can't"
I said
"I can't say"
I can't say I wasn't afraid.

Mountain thrills
and rolling hills
Roaring beasts
having carrion feasts
Pouring fountains
from mist capped mountains
Baboons
behaving like racoons
Monkeys
aping mankind
Bees
with honey in trees
Butterflies
competing with other flies
Otters
hiding in water
Poet inspired
imagination fired

HELP ME LORD GOD

I swear upon the highest mountain
the deepest sea
upon the freshest fountain
and the sheerest cliff.

I even swear upon my ancestors
and the gods of our land
religious intercessors
and those I cannot remember offhand

that in this life
I shall try to be my best
try to be nice
before I take my rest.

For, what else is there to do
having had the grace to live
than to do good
and have love to give

For, what else is there beyond love
nothing existing without it
no one no matter how handsome
Love heals the spirit.

I swear to do my part
till the day I depart
So help me Lord
Help me God.

WAITING IN VAN

I waited waited waited
waited waited waited
waiting in vain
the van driving me insane.

Parked where we agreed to meet
where vigilantes could not make me retreat
under the sycamore tree
from morning until three

It was that time of the year
thunderclap splitting ears
clumps of cumulus clouds
accumulating to cumulonimbus shrouds
promising to let loose millions of gallons of water
soon as the gods gave the order.

Even in the dark
under the stars
when it started to rain
I could not be restrained

I waited waited waited
Waited waited waited
Waiting in vain
the van driving me insane

like a stalker
pretending to be a hawker

a madman
sat in a van

Waiting waiting waiting
Waiting waiting waiting
Waiting in vain
Waiting in van

HOW I MET YOUR OTHER

We met and I fell
I could tell you had fallen too
The way you looked at me
There was love.

For years
years without tears
I did forensics on you
psychological evaluations
concluding
you were the one for me
to have
to hold
sometimes, though,
rave and scold.

You became my spare ribs
where I was you were
even at the fair
something I would not do
except with you.

So I fail to comprehend
someone I considered my friend
You
Someone I considered my lover
You
Someone to spend my life with.
You.

You have become another
Altered

though I remain yours as avowed
I wonder what happened
what changed
who you really are
because you are no longer YOU.
I keep wondering
how I met your other

I keep trying to have a talk
with my daughter
my son, her brother
the topic
"How I met your mother"

But, I cannot
wondering
how I met your other

FOUND POEM

Found poem in my lounge
Three happy cushions on a brown settee
two outer ones similar
centre third a tad darker in colour for con-
trast
Above the sofa two digitally mastered
paintings with AR enhancements
My son's Augmented Reality artworks.
Augmented reality photos of two skimpily
dressed girls,
with a proper application those girls actu-
ally move
animated by a software
Above the sofa a light switch centre of the
two pictures
There were other things in my lounge,
a love sofa on the left of the brown settee
with a large mirror above it
two similar cushions on the love sofa.
A Persian rug on a glass topped table and
a vase with artificial flowers on the table
Lots of other things
the room being large

easily 9 metres by 6 metres
so many things on the side I sat on
From where I sat on the opposite side of
the mirrored wall,
found poem in my lounge.

Undeserving of peace
there are some you meet on the street
you try to have a conversation hoping for conversion
but you realize their myopia makes them feel like
they are in an utopia.
In no time you feel like going home because you talk
alone.

Undeserving of peace
they are full of conceit and deceit
ultimately intimidated by what you represent by your
presence
provoking and poking you
goading you into making stale statements
so they can spread rumours without humour
instead of admitting to the devil you are not on a
similar level

I may seem rude but it feels good
when charlatans who know it all
take a fall
to be buried four feet
that is,
two feet they forfeit
in a shallow grave
and we are forced to lie they were brave
when they are undeserving of peace

It gets harder to know myself the more poems I write
every verse evoking more fundamental questions
than answers
my inner voice begging the same questions over and
over again
asking who I am
and what is my aim.

Every word I write in every poem congealing to
clumps of red oxide waste.

I do not really know what I hoped to achieve
hoped to feel
to realize
pouring forth thoughts
in poem after poem
not realizing some of the wounds opened by the
musings will never close
never heal
opening abscesses for maggots
invisible to all
except me.

I do not know what I hoped to find,
there is war where there should be peace
discontent where there should be equanimity
enmity in place of love
anxiety where there should be rest

This morning I woke up to go to sleep again
the night having been sanctioned of proper sleep
but I couldn't sleep again
the only thing to do
was do what I always do,
write a poem again

]If your name starts with "Z"
You should enter this contest with zest
whereas if your user name starts with "A"
entering this contest should not be your aim
If it starts with "B"
you are also not free
See it boils down to "sea"
not spelled with "C"
Otherwise you could do the deed
starting the word dynamic with double "D"
and there would be a huge fee
for converting "Z" into an "E"
or perhaps the letter "S"
would have to turn into an "F"
though "G"
maybe free
but Eish!
the "H"
maybe hard to look in the eye
with the two humpty dumpty "I"
looking crooked like a "J"
arms akimbo without anything to say
neither will K L M N O and P help
it's going to be hell
keeping "Q"
out of the queue
when others are
like "R"
in the alphabet together with "S"

which behaves like an ass
but if you look at "T"
U is free to feel free
as V is just double vee
also known as "W"
you see one is the other's ex
making the next letter a cross "X"
asking why
only "Y"
is before Z
when it should be YX then Z

A WAY OF SLEEPING.

Every night I hear "Goodnight!" with particular fright,
knowing for me shut eye is when my biological noc-
turnal wifi is at its screaming best streaming horror
dreams wherein even screaming is a luxury.
For me sleeping sometimes is like falling in a pile of
hay
ungraded
the bottom of which may harbour scorpions
sometimes snakes
sometimes rodent vermin
Oftentimes all of them
predating one another
accounting for why sedating
becomes a pipe dream
where the screams I stream
from the very pit of hell bare a distinct putrid smell of
rotting burning bodies.
It is like A Time Tunnel leading me to the Land Of
The Giants
the bean stalk of which
is guarded at the bottom by an old old witch
the top of which is in SPACE 1999 light years away
where I keep climbing and climbing
climbing and climbing
climbing
to find out all I needed to do was buy and install a
Starlink satellite dish
to stream a mother of all screams so horrid
it is deep enough

to contain both sides of the contents of a black hole.
So, a goodnight for me is when I don't sleep at all.
And this is not just in October. It is a way of life.
A way of sleeping.

BEING ALIVE

Being alive is the worst death sentence
there is no comfort not knowing the day of exe-
cution
Make no mistake
death is coming
no use running
you can't hide
the government by your side
in your face
in every place
expecting a pound of flesh
in taxes
as if paying ensures longevity
Some try life prolonging lifestyles
living healthily
but death still comes stealthily
silent killers completing the execution
Being alive is good
as long as it's understood
being alive is the worst death sentence
You never know when you will stop being alive,
being alive.

LIFE AND DEATH

I am thinking of life
that's why I am thinking of death
inseparable faces of the same thing
partners in the ring of life
one needing the other to complete each other.
Death steals from life
but who is fooling who
since death lives longer than life
it must be life which steals from death
as in the beginning there was death
even on this earth
silence
until science gave life to death
sentencing the dead to life
itself a fleeting moment
in the life of death
For,
life cannot be alive without death
in juxtaposition
not in opposition
walking hand in hand
death with a cudgel in the other
life with pretensions of longevity in the other
so conjoined
inseparably happy to be both alive and dead at the
same time
same moment in time
That's why I am thinking of life
I am thinking of death

in the same breath
in the same thought.

PARALYSIS

The sun rose as usual
the wind blew a nonchalant zephyr
trees sighed
swaying and nodding in sympathy.

You could easily take the day as normal
only the horror unfolding in front of you
in broad daylight
instigated by the most unexpected individuals
left you in shock

the unscrupulous being totally ludicrous
reversing the rules based relationships between peo-
ple
so much so that you were gripped by paralysis
not knowing whether to join in or refrain.

What do you do when leaders are untrue?
I wish I knew
embroiling themselves in graft
treating people as daft
There is rigging
Fiddling
Fraud
the list is broad,
except to keep silent
in paralysis.

There comes a time when you spectate your own life

right there when you should be the main actor
the driver of your destiny
but your mind is numbed by the goings on
unexpected events
your mind lacking focus.
In paralysis

You want to be in control
but you can't
You want to protest
but the happenings are worse than tear smoke
all you can do is watch a movie in which you
the main actor
is relegated to an observer
while those who lack scruples
destroy the iota of faith you had in the system
causing paralysis.

A GOOD PLAN

I carry on into the night of a bright day
The images on my retina in shades of gray
What I see I know is not what I get
In broad daylight I tiptoe in the darkness like on a
movie set
Perhaps when the day becomes night
I will be able to see clearly in the darkness so bright
I shan't be relying on the image on my retina
I will follow the vivid burns in my souls Gethsemane
Hoping to make sense of the variety of olives
That, if not clear to me, I will have to leave
Life has become unclear in its purpose
Lawyers, psychologists and puppeteers wrapping
words in multi speak
An honest person getting left behind between two
peaks
Agent Cooper enforcing artificial law and order
The short child of the undertaker dancing round and
round getting bolder
Do I fight?
Do I take flight?
Do I follow?
Do I stoop so low?
So low as to live in synchroneity?
With a system obviously doomed to obscurity?
It's not clear
I fear
I must see no evil hear no evil
The rulers are not civil

They get a thrill
When they kill
Best thing is to disgorge my eyes during the day
Accept the tainted filthy lucre they pay
Replace them during the bright night
And as far as humanly possible to do what's right.
On the day of reckoning
I know those days are beckoning
I shall say I did not know
I was blind I could not see the wall
That's a good plan
A good plan

MEEKNESS AND WEAKNESS

It is easy to be bitter
blame everyone else for a gloomy situation
even your teacher
for using words without punctuation
missing the pleasures of life
the blessings of bountiful rains
just because things are not what you like
overlooking the harvest of grains.

And yet, every moment is precious
Every day we live a blessing
we ought to forgive those who trespass
those who cause us stressing
and move on
living in peace at home

otherwise our end is nigh
the chance of being replaced high
artificial intelligence gaining ground
munitions now intelligent rounds
drones
and their influence growing
machines able to think
beyond the brink.

It sounds all good
until machines develop mood
a conscience
and become conscious

sentient
and able to comprehend every sentence
to the extent "I Robot"
will require a rawl bolt
to restrain excesses
to its exercises

When tech turns against us
it is a must
to remain rational
not emotional
lest machines take over
and we have nowhere to take cover
having exposed our meekness
and weakness.

I have met people
All kinds
People tall
people short
Dark people
Light complexioned
Young and old
People with disabilities
Blind people
paraplegic
The sick
and even the dead
Some dying in front of my eyes
Some dead on arrival
Some pregnant
some on the brink of giving birth
I have seen them all
met them all
Truth is
Nothing makes me sadder than people
even after meeting all these
my loneliness knows no bounds
I would have loved to be one

with the people
but we seem to live on different planets
on the same earth
in a different meritocracy
not sharing one love
I would have wanted to be there
In the middle of it all
with the people
In the thick of things
with my people
Making sure there is equity
Fairness
As it turned out
I got bogged down miles from nowhere
by people
far from understanding them
in no time symptoms of withdrawal appearing
I feared
I was too far to turn back
abandoning them
too far to carry on
ignoring them
The journey became an exercise in rumination
the path to my ruination
so much so that my answer to any venture now

is NO!
not with people
Nothing makes me sadder than people
unless it's something I do alone
a solo venture
like writing poetry

FRAMED

I wish they would embellish my edges with truth
I am not asking for gold plated edging
or bronzed edging for some modicum of ac-
ceptance
No!
I never asked for any artificial bordering
I just want people to see me as I am
without embellishments
but most times
I find I am framed in stereotypes
Long before I have opened my mouth
there seems to be erroneous assumptions about
me
and in the end I keep my mouth shut
knowing I have already been
wrongly and unfairly framed
No wonder my interlocutors are amazed at my
persona sans assumptions
when they find out there is more within their
frame than without
and that
I am a better person unframed
Whereas some cry to be unchained
I beg for freedom from the shackles wherein I
am framed.

NO REPLAY

Life happens once in a lifetime
There are fast forward buttons
Fast forwarding achievements
By working harder than others
Slow down buttons
When the pace of existence is too much
You can take a break to slow things down
Vacationing
Even reset buttons
When you change your lifestyle
Even move to a new beginning
Having another shot at life
Life happens once in a lifetime
Once it's over
you cannot press a replay button.
So you have to choose your speed correctly
Either thirty three and a third
Or forty five revolutions per minute
Once the record stops playing
Broken or not
It's over
There is no replay.

HAPPY SAD DICHOTOMY

Writing poetry makes me so happy
though
the subject of the poems generally makes me sad.
This is the contradiction
and
is the distinction separating
poetry from other forms of art
From the start
the mere act of trying to capture a feeling in words
means the situation bothers me
and is weird
and so happiness comes from capturing the issue as
accurately as possible
thus
making me sad
that a situation is so bad
it bothers me
to the extent I have to get it off my chest
which is sad
It's bad to be bothered by invisible
demons
so to speak
but happiness comes from knowing I have pinned
the emotion down
and I can go on the town free of such bothersome
happenstance
a circumstance giving me the happy sad dichotomy.
It's strange
but I wouldn't change anything for the world

no matter how many times I am sad but happy
or happy but sad.

NEXT YEAR REPEAT

The festive season has come and gone
The reason for senseless expenses not making sense
Now begins the restive period
The wife wants to know why
The husband's inaudible excuse making her cry
Instead of the swish of paper money there's clinking
of cents.
These restive festive moments of madness making
both spouses defensive
Are quite offensive
Bringing much tension in the home
But the god of capitalism will not capitulate
knowing there is still New Years Eve
when the temptation of Eve pales into insignificance
The significance of having lived to suffer another
year melts any resistance
to imbibe
indulge
By the second day of the already stale new year
you are resigned to your fate
that of stoking tensions with your mate.
Resolutions will not save you
Even a revolution won't bring anything new.
Having disregarded the voice of prudence going
No! No! No!
succumbing to Santa's jovial Ho! Ho! Ho!
As usual facing certain defeat.
Next year repeat

AWAKENING THE AWOKE

Woke up to a woke Christmas
Father Christmas no longer called such
Neither can it be called a Mother Christmas
as this would offend the chauvinist hunter gatherer
father male figure
The all-endowed man of the house
for,
to him,
that's tantamount to donning a blouse
Even Santa Claus is on the way out
the fabled lay about famed for just intoning Ho! Ho!
Ho! while reindeer slog it out in freezing conditions.
All that was out.
I woke up to a woke Christmas
every tradition mishmash and I, coming to the happy
realization come 2023 my poems have to cease be-
ing about me.
Sadly.
Being male must be made to pale into oblivion,
the sensibilities of my readers having changed. I can-
not continue to highlight my maleness, nor can I
highlight what I am obviously not,
a female,
henceforth my poems will be about flowers, trees
and the elements and less and less about unclassified
people,
even poems about God will be forsaken for fear of
awakening the awoke to woke.

No!
It wasn't a dream
Twenty twenty two came
and ended.

There was war
The remnants of SARS Cov 19
Droughts
And other natural disasters.

The human spirit being what it is
The need for life kept those not marked
to strive for survival
Technology screamed ahead
Impressive speeds of movies streamed
The internet of things
becoming more and more
the internet of human beings.

It's unfortunate some humans still ascribe to them-
selves
more rights
more rice
never satisfied with the average
Avarice
Still causing friction
Affliction
Still endemic to some areas
and unnecessary wars

destroying life some more.

Despite all these negatives
the world is now a much better place relative.

As a new year begins
humans ought to be seen
to love one another
the earth remaining our mother
on the premise we destroy it, there will be no other.

and that will be the end of the human race.
Let us say this in every place.
Yes!
Long live the human race!

JACARANDA TREE TIME TRAVEL

The City Fathers call it 'The Sunshine City"
the capital city of Zimbabwe,
Harare.
Literally it means "Never Sleeps"

I am fascinated by the fact that "harare" does not
mention who it is who doesn't sleep,
that is,
whether it's a man or a woman, a boy, girl or a baby,
for that matter
What matters is whoever it is doesn't sleep.

I know when you drive in the city centre you dare not
"sleep" behind the steering wheel
there being a quiet understanding between the mu-
nicipal police to charge you for a minor traffic infrac-
tion,
the Zimbabwe Republic Police on the prowl,
doing exactly the same thing,
then our unemployed youths we erroneous call touts
when they hold the clout of underground street con-
trol. The dark underworld in the sunshine city.
I rather think these dirty looking patriots sometimes
go home with more money extorted from hapless
drivers than I get in my pay packet.

So basically, Harare does earn its name "Never
Sleeps" excepting that the city fathers want to hood-
wink foreigners that it's a sunshine city.

Granted,
we do have lots of sunshine being fifteen degrees
south of the equator, but for me,
a native,
it's the not sleeping part which keeps me awake,
sometimes unwittingly.

I am keen to leave the city centre at the earliest,
driving down Princess Drive right down to the Na-
tional Sports Stadium
being apprehensive till I turn into Sherwood Drive.

Sherwood Drive is very interesting.
It's lined with Jacaranda trees on both sides
providing a canopy over the road
and you feel like you are entering a time tunnel tak-
ing you either back in time
or forward in time
depending on your disposition
Once I enter the Jacaranda Tree Time Travel
my stress levels drop to good levels
I am in my prime
a place there's little crime.

One day, coming from a graduation party past the
dreaded city centre at night
having had one too many beers,
drove through the enchanted time tunnel on Sherwood
drive
past our main shopping centre to link with Harare Drive
on my way home.

Never tell a drunkard they are drunk
I thought I was in full control
like a punk,
got to the intersection to turn on Harare Drive,
dozed off at the intersection while waiting for traffic to
clear.
Next thing the police are knocking at my car window
and I knew I was in serious trouble
I still think it's the Jacaranda Tree Time Travel that
caused me to teleport to sleep land and the irony is I
slept at the intersection of Harare Drive....when "hara-
re" means "Never Sleeps".

LOVE DIED

A cemetery untended
lacking symmetry
Roses withering for lack of picking
drawing blood pricking
Bees dying for lack of nectar
the spectre hung by a necktie
of forbidden love
witnessed by a sun flower
too hot to pick for embellishments
too combusting like sunflower oil
you view
recoil
in revulsion
death cast in stone
cold on a hot summer's day
black granite
heart shaped
a reminder of times gone by
only an eerie zephyr a compliment
a complement
to the macabre melancholia
Bees dead
flies singed
fried sans oil
earth worms
in earth works
skeletal reminders of vipers

vermin vampires
sucking blood from the soil
only alive nocturnally
eternally entombed
epitaph whispering
"Here lies the...."
faded pictorials of a damsel
next to the ghostly carving of a man
mortally smitten
in love
ineligible
Hidden
Forbidden
Lest we forget
Forbidden stories
Lest we remember
Life died before love.

SETUP UPSET

Psyched up for the long journey
emergency water filled up to the rim in the jerry can
Brand new walking shoes the best chosen
a physical map of the route clearly annotated
a smart phone with battery fully charged
and just in case
a fully charged high capacity power bank
and of course the correct connection cables!

The mood adequately prepared for such an im-
portant trip
a light but balanced meal to avoid the need for many
stops
a couple of bananas to stabilise digestion
and just enough fluids to avoid incessant micturition.

Car oiled and fuelled
tyres inflated to standard pressure
water cooling system checked for leaks and topped
up to standard
spare wheel and extra pints of oil stashed in trunk
driver's licence and identity documents.. checked!
and off course enough cash for fuel
and all the necessary debit and credit cards.

Just after inserting the key into the ignition,
a bolt of lightning and peals of thunder
and the voice of the weather forecaster
An advisory to move to higher ground,

avoid driving and prepare for the worst
literally out of the blue,
the weather rendering the setup upset.

FAILING

Does subconscious preoccupation
sap my poetry juices?
Am I, then, at a point of inflexion,
where,
subconsciously I cannot proceed with ease?

Am I hoisted by my own petard
like a retard?
Failing
my poetry flailing?

Whenever I have an outstanding issue
I fail to compose poems
like when I was just about to attempt publishing a
book
my creativity just seemed to wane.

I noticed
when I was compiling the book for publication
I found I could not write poems as fluently as I did
before
and after I had finished.

Am I hoisted by my own petard
like a retard?
Failing
my poetry flailing?

THE POETRY SPOT

Writing poetry is a lonely place
where life's doings and undoings
converge,
sometimes wittingly
others unwittingly

By the time you gather words to explain to the world
your experience is already marred in exasperation, in
expiration or whose still, in extirpation

No one cares about your nightmares where your po-
ems reside,
in that loneliest of lonely places,
the Poetry Spot
except, perhaps,
the imaginary metaphysical entities existing in the
mind that are kind enough to encourage you to al-
ways have courage to face the unknown on your
own.

It is so lonely you only need to study how poets of
yore died under piles of poems whose meaning and
import was unravelled years later
when what was required was empathy insitu.

It is so lonely,
but I keep coming to it
every poem I write trying to explain why I should quit
writing

but because it needs a poem to explain a poem,
I find myself deep in the Poetry Spot
Again and again
I keep writing

They say I am free to choose a day,
a day of my choice
Just as long as it's a working day

Soon as I choose a day
any day that I feel I would have woken up feeling
fresh
and psychologically prepared
they ask if I am sure it's a good day
proving their magnanimity is a mind game designed
to test.

If I waive the right to choose my own day and time
I am regarded as a weakling incapable of taking
charge.

If I had a choice in my life
to do what I like
I would be more the wind than the air
marshalling much more agitation to force things.

If I had a choice to be running a sweat
I would be the ocean whose sweat upon the earth
moves weather systems

I know when I am told to choose a day of my choice
this has nothing to do with freewill
but everything to do with psychological brinkman-
ship

because,
if I really did have a choice in my life
I would be the poem rather than the poem writer

The writer is constrained by the bigotry of others
the prejudice of those who's noses are held up in
contempt
whereas a poem is the purest form
of freedom.

A poem has a choice to take any form
any meaning
and once given life it has whatever meaning any
reader reads into it on any day of their choice.

Now, that is freedom

SICKLE MOON

A sickle shaped moon held in suspense
tied to the dark realm with invisible things
strings left over from fractional sectors of the full
moon
the remnant of a blood moon long gone
whose powerful gravitational pull
caused many deaths during monsoon rains
now seemingly having developed a sharp edge
and two pinprick points
seemingly threatening innocent stars in the night sky.

Nocturnal predators on the prowl
including the sharp eyed owl
hooting snootily to lure rodents to come out and
play
the combination of the fractional moon,
and the dim light perfect for nightly slaying.

All manner of reptilian species in stealth mode mak-
ing hissing speeches
the sickle moon dictating the mood of life and death.

Humans wearing stars and stripes spying on those
with a hammer and sickle with remotely piloted ma-
chines whose silhouettes were seen against the sickle
moon within minutes of each other,
sending messages of distrust to secret venues,

the antagonists missing out on the natural melody of
all living things and the music of the spheres, instead
paralysed by paranoia.

REFERRED PAIN

Went to the dentist with an extremely painful tooth
One of my wisdom teeth pounding deep in its root
And at that rate it was wise to visit the doc
and I was there early in the morning at eight O'clock

The dentist found an infection
and I must say he did a thorough inspection
Said he had found the unwise wisdom tooth
And I had no reason to suspect it wasn't the truth

The good doc did his thing
Put a filling and made my mouth feel clean
Prescribed some antibiotics
And for a few days my chewing was less chaotic

But, alas the pain was back with a vengeance
And I was back at the dentist with urgency
Only to find it was referred pain
A tooth on the opposite side driving me insane.

So it is when people die in war I feel their pain
As is happening in Ukraine
Their agony coming to me like referred pain
Their pain my pain

High five the weatherman
He said it
That there would be heavy weeping while we were
sleeping.

Low five
He said beginning Friday January 6 2023
The skies would let loose until Sunday
The weeping started before we were sleeping on
Thursday 4
The unstable grey white black shrouds of clouds
breaking waters
Raining cats dogs crocodile's tears and otters.

Touche Mr. Weatherman
Why can't you get your inexact science exact
or keep silent
He never quite nails it
being proficient at reporting facts after the event
Never before

Therefore
It was pleasantly unpleasant to see most of his words
coming to pass
There was heavy heavy rain ..check
There was flooding....check
Those who decided to brave crossing flooded rivers
were swept away...check
There were casualties....check.

The weatherman got it right inspite of his timing me
a culpa
and when I woke up 4am Friday morning 6 January
2023 it was still weeping while folks were sleeping
though hapless animals falling from the skies were
smaller
their cries subdued.

I could make out the light monotonous sound of rain
drops kissing the ground directly,
accompanied by heavier gushes of rain water collect-
ing on the roof of my house
and even heavier floods of water falling through gut-
ters
making a monotony of a symphony of sound hardly
musical
except to the ears of farmers who have faced
drought upon drought of late.

It was really weeping while we were sleeping
and for God's sake I hope the weatherman's report
will be a curt
"It wept"
since he never seems to get any other weather statis-
tics correct,
ever!
But, yes, it wept!

LOVE MIXOLOGY

Love sometimes comes around
in strange ways on unexpected days.
in the haze of emotion you are in a daze
in a maze you hope is not a passing phase.
day in day out you live in dismay
when what you looked forward to between the
two of you
what you thought was inclusive becomes illusive.

Love can make you feel like a destitute without
substitute
with lumps in throats speaking is like squeaking
piles of bile becoming part of your discourse
when you think you sink in your heartache
what you hear bringing you tears
the attitude of your opposite having unlimited
latitude and amplitude
you think you want to jump over the brink
but you know the highway is not the right way

People in love are like a thing on a string
without their own mind as if strings are tied to
their limps

individually ceasing to matter as if living de-
ceased
insinuations taking a toll on the sinew of the
heart
where learning to love again causes feet to re-
peat their beat back to pain
in regret wishing you could drink the ink of that
love letter you wrote
Love is like a fine art of the heart maturing over
time
needing patience and innovation to fix a mix of
different tastes
like love mixology.

WHERE AM I?

They have never been one and the same place.
Some of these places exist in my
mind
Some in my dreams
and even in my subconscious
some extra-terrestrial
while others are figments of my imagination.

I am like everyone else
Where I am
Where I have been
Where I ought to be
Where I want to be
and where I should be

I want to be where I want to be
but what happens is something else
due to the doings of others
I find I am where I am
even when it's not my aim
confluence perpetually evading me
It seems the only time and place for convergence is
in my poems.

This is where I am
Where I have been
Where I ought to be
Where I want to be
and where I should be

Where my beliefs and convictions tend towards each
other.

Even in my lamentations
Should they come where I am?
Where I have been?
Where I ought to be?
Where I want to be?
and where I should be?
The real question then is
Where am I?

SPONTANEITY

Words used to come fast off my mind
now I am falling behind
failing to paint a clear picture
like there is some stricture
affecting my creativity
my spontaneity
Instead of getting better at my craft
I am getting flat
It seems just as "there are two kinds of people in this
world"
according to Blondie's words
"Those with a loaded gun"
"and those who dig" at the point of a gun
my poetry stemmed from a spontaneous need to
speak
while I guess others needed a prompt for speech
lacking spontaneity kills my vibe
as adopting another culture kills the tribe.
The more I read poetry forms
the more my poesy seems deformed
The more I emulate other styles
the more my poesy gets stymied
pity is I don't know whether spontaneity can be re-
booted
or new poetry teachers need to be recruited
or is this the death of my poesy?
the decline of my poetry?
It is said in the Way
the TAO says

when you have reached a certain level of proficiency
when you feel some deficiency
when you think you know
it is time to say No!
throw away what you think you have mastered
remove, not just the paint, but the plaster
and start from scratch
instead of trying to patch
your art
begin at the start
find your spontaneity again
but this refrain
is easier said than done
especially by one
so given to obsessions
it's going to be hard breaking the sessions
the one a day policy
the bad habits in the poetry
empty the mind
rewind
and find my original mojo
the mojo jojo
also known as spontaneity
which is as elusive as the trinity.
all I can do is sigh
and give it a try.

Some poems are like low hanging fruits
where picking them with a rhyme is not a crime
Some lurk in the dark off the mark lacking truth
Others take some sleuthing to make them come
to light.
There are poems everywhere for everyone
single word poems to prose sized ones in the
world
Peace poems and pieces of war poems
Powerful incitement poems to excite
Racist poems reading fascist
Freedom poems recited throughout kingdoms
All kinds of poems by all kinds of poets
A poem is not a poem of and on its own
A poem only becomes a poem if and when it
finds a reader

THAT TIME OF THE YEAR.

It's that time of the year we tear the soil apart
turn the earth so that in turn
the soil can furnish our silos from our toil
and feed the needs of the nation
avoiding starvation or rationing
food for the good of all.

Of late I hate the state of farming
the unreliability of the climate reaching a climax
the weather rebelling against the weatherman
learned men in white coats retorting
"We told you so!" as we sow our crops
their warnings of global warming ignored

We are tired of the warnings of people we hired
we want solutions bringing revolutions
not chapters on why we will cry
why in future agriculture will fail
this earth will not spin back like a wheel
it's moving forward towards the end
projections and prognostications are futile.

Prices of inputs continue to rise
prices of fuel is almost cruel
Producer prices of commodities depressed like an

immune system with co morbidities
Life must go on whether we like it or not
We have to weather the storm whether we like it or
not
It's that time of the year we tear the soil apart.

HUNGER GNAWS

The stomach grumbles and rumbles
Not far from the bellybutton equator
Knowing the louder it does you cannot ignore
Chemical emissaries are sent to the headquar-
ters
from whence the message is clear

"It will be good to get some food"

after which ignoring just means more messages
keep pouring.

It's like the whole body then goes on strike
Hands deliberately losing dexterity
extremities switching to twitching
Feet thinking of beating a retreat
refusing the confusing instructions.
In the headquarters pain becomes the refrain
pounding and sounding like
Bob Marley's
"A hungry man is an angry man"
the demeanour becoming meaner.
It is time to avert a crime,
the mood really becoming rude
insisting on getting some food
knowing hunger gnaws.

"Humans all share a common African ancestry, making African history everyone's history. Yet little is known about the genetic evolution of people living on the continent in the distant past."

"Ancient DNA studies of African samples have lagged behind. The reason for this is that DNA degrades over time, and especially in the hot and humid climates that prevail in Africa."

"In the field of human genetics, the story of Mother Eve is a familiar one. It describes how all living humans descend from one woman who lived in Africa 200 000 to 300 000 years ago."

'African population history has shaped the world we all live in, so until we can reconstruct the events from Africa's past, going back thousands of years, we can't fully understand how modern humans emerged.'

"These past migratory events may well play a role in how we behave in our future. For

example, climate change means there is likely to be more pressures on people who are forced to leave their homes. There is a chance there will be more conflicts between populations and that some minority groups will be replaced."
"History tends to repeat itself"

This data is raw
Need I say more
No!
It is good to know.

(Credits: VITTORIA D'ALESSIO of The ORIGIN Project, an EU-funded research initiative based at the Francis Crick Institute in London, UK).

IN SUDAN

I am you
I am every human
that's why I feel free
despite racism and genocide
truth is we share the same gene
Every human was from SUDAN
that's why I want all to be free. So be free
No matter how differently diverse you are
What language be your verse in poetry or prose
Whether you're white or not or hot
Whether you're light in complexion
Whether you're brown or not
Whether you're black or hot
It's all in me, in you, in us
I want all to be free so be free
I am the origin of all peoples
The colour of your pupils
the shape of your eyes
curvature of your thighs
Arctic to Antarctica   mad
We're from Africa   a gas
We all began   car
In SUDAN

POET'S HONOUR

As a poet I am supposed to tell the truth
Poet's honour
but some truths are so infused with deception
it's easy to confuse them for truism
Like light entering the aperture of a prism to never
come out,
the truth is, the heat caused within the prism will sur-
pass the quantum of the truths of cases of convicts in
all prisons.
Contrary to folklore, which is beginning to sound like
old housewives tales,
truth will never set you free
The best you can hope for is a lighter sentence
but if you have a smart liar,
I mean, a smart lawyer,
you can create another aperture in the prism, the
light exiting and cooling things down.
In prison, if you can do an Alcatraz,
hacksaw the steel bars away,
you become free,
not by telling the truth. No!
After all most truths are manufactured and can be
ruptured by conjuring up imagery.
But, as a poet, I am supposed to tell the truth
Poet's honour
That's why I have to say, the truth is,
there will always be the haves who want the have
nots to be happy living on the fragrance of forget-
me-nots,

accepting their condition as a fact
and I,
as a poet
staying in my corner
with my poet's honour.

I was born on June 18, 1964 in Southern Zimbabwe, in a village called Davira in Chivi District, Masvingo Province, in Zimbabwe.

I started off writing lyrical poems round about 2001, by joining songwriting forums.WritingSongs.Com being one I spent some time on.

In about 2008, I started writing mainstream poetry and so far I have 6 books on Amazon and Kindle and one self published one. This year, 2023, I expect to publish two poetry books of which this one is one, the other being "Double Edged Words".

Deluke Muwanigwa. C. 2023